Presented to

_____

From

_____

Date

_____

The
TODDLERS®
Bible

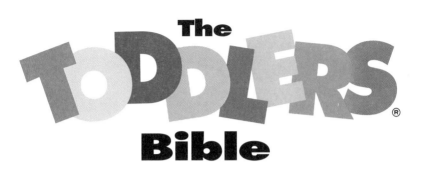

The TODDLERS Bible

V. Gilbert Beers

Illustrated by

Carole Boerke

VICTOR BOOKS

A DIVISION OF SCRIPTURE PRESS PUBLICATIONS INC.
USA CANADA ENGLAND

Published in Wheaton, Illinois by Victor Books/Scripture Press.

ISBN 0-89693-077-7

Printed in the United States of America
8 9 10 11 12 — 98 97 96 95 94 93

Contents

To Parent and Teacher

Something wonderful happens at the toddler age. Your child enters doorways of adventure through the world of words and visual wonders. He learns to talk, she learns to walk, and they learn to love God or ignore Him. A lifetime of knowing and loving God is formed, or missed, at this early age. A lifetime of Bible reading, Bible study, Bible application begins here. What you do with your toddler is for all of life, or for all eternity.

Above all else, our purpose in the Toddlers Bible is to help your child fall in love with the Word of God. It is not the whole Bible, because your toddler is not yet ready for the whole Bible. That will come later. But your toddler is ready to start building a delight in the Word, a hunger to learn it, a passion to read it. This is the age to begin building that delight, or hunger, or passion. Next year may be too late.

The Toddlers Bible is filled with beautiful art, words within the reach of your toddler, ideas that toddlers can grasp. It comes not from a book of theory, but from almost 40 years of practical parenting which built that delight in the Word in my own children and grandchildren. It really works!

The Toddlers Bible walks through the great stories, or adventures, of the Bible step by step, leading your toddler in tiny steps, not giant leaps. It speaks with softness, yet remains faithful to the key teachings of the Word of God.

Since your toddler cannot yet read, he or she will depend on you to a "read-to-me" experience. But you will find it the richest experience of your lifetime. Of course, your "learning-to-read" child will enjoy the Toddlers Bible, and I think you will too.

Please start today on one of the most rewarding journeys you will ever walk—through the Word with your toddler and God. You'll be ever grateful that you did.

—*V. Gilbert Beers*

Creation

Oh! Look at the beautiful sky!
Do you see the moon?
Do you see the stars?

Nothing was there before. The sky
was dark. It was empty.

Then God spoke. Wonderful
things happened. Our beautiful
world appeared. The sun shined.

Birds sang. Animals were
everywhere. Only God could
make all these things.

15

God Makes Adam and Eve

"I need someone to take care of My beautiful world," God said.

God made a man. He called the
man Adam.

Then God made a woman. Adam
and Eve took care of God's world.

God also made you and me. He
is a wonderful God, isn't He?

The Garden of Eden

Eden was a beautiful garden home.
God made it for Adam and Eve.

"You may eat anything here," God said. "But you can't eat THAT fruit on THAT tree!"

21

"That's the best fruit of all," Satan
said. So Adam and Eve ate some of it.

Now Adam and Eve were sad. They had disobeyed God. They had to leave Eden.

Noah Builds a Big Boat

"Build a big boat," God said. Noah
loved God. He would obey God.

Look at that boat that Noah built!
It is bigger than three houses.

"Put animals on the boat," God said.
So Noah put many animals on it.

Noah and his family went on the boat.
That's what God told them to do.

God Sends a Big Flood

One day it began to rain. It rained and rained and rained.

Water went over the trees. It went over the mountains.

But God took care of Noah and his
family. They were safe on the big boat.

"Thank You, God," Noah said. He was glad now that he obeyed God.

The Tower of Babel

One day some men made a tall
tower. It would make them look
important.

These men were very proud.
But God did not like this.

God made them stop building the
tower. He made them go away to
many places.

Now they did not look so important.
Now they needed God.

Isaac Is Born

Abraham wanted a son. He was
sad when he saw other children.

But Abraham was 100 years old.
He and Sarah were too old to
have a baby.

"I WILL give you a son," God
promised. Shhh. Do you hear
their baby boy crying?

Abraham and Sarah named their
new baby Isaac. "Thank You, God,"
said Abraham.

Esau and Jacob Are Born

"Please give us a baby," Isaac and Rebekah prayed.

God heard their prayers.
He gave them TWO sons.
They were TWINS!

Esau would become a great
hunter. But God had special
plans for Jacob.

Jacob's family would be called
Israelites. Much of our Bible is
about them.

Esau Sells His Birthright

One day Esau went hunting.
His brother Jacob stayed home
to work.

Jacob cooked some stew to eat.
When Esau came home he
was hungry.

45

"Give me some stew," said Esau.
"Give me your birthright,"
said Jacob.

So Esau traded his right to lead his family. All he got was a bowl of stew.

Isaac Will Not Fight

God gave Isaac many good things.
But the Philistines nearby grew
jealous.

The Philistines filled Isaac's wells
with dirt. So Isaac had no water. But
Isaac would not fight them.

Isaac moved. The people there
stole his wells. But Isaac would
not fight them.

God liked what Isaac did. "I will
give you many good things,"
God said.

Jacob Tricks His Father

Jacob and Esau were Isaac's twin boys. But Esau was a few minutes older.

So Esau would lead the family
when Isaac died.

One day Jacob tricked his father.
Isaac gave his blessing to Jacob.

Now Jacob would lead the family
instead of Esau.

Jacob's Dream

One day Jacob went on a trip.
He went far, far away from home.

Jacob was very tired.
That night Jacob had a dream.

In this dream, angels walked
up and down on a stairway.
Then God spoke to Jacob.

"I will do good things for you,"
God said. "And I will do good
things for You," said Jacob.

Jacob Meets Rachel

Look! Do you see that beautiful lady? Rachel helps her father with his sheep.

Jacob sees Rachel too. He wants
to meet her. How do you think
he will do it?

Now you know. Jacob gives some water to Rachel's sheep.

Some day Jacob and Rachel will get married.

Joseph's Brothers Sell Him

Oh, no! No one would sell his brother. But Joseph's brothers did.

Joseph's brothers did not like him.
Some even wanted to kill him.

Then some men said they would buy Joseph. They would make him a slave.

So Joseph's brothers sold him.
They were very bad brothers,
weren't they?

God Helps Joseph

Poor Joseph. He is in jail.
Someone lied about him. So he
was put in jail. Joseph was sad.

But one night the king had a dream.
"What does it mean?" he shouted.
No one could tell him.

69

Then God told Joseph what it
meant. Joseph told the king. That
made the king happy.

"You are a wise man," said the king.
"You will rule over my people."

Joseph's Secret

Joseph has a secret.
No one else knows.
Joseph's brothers do not know.

His brothers have come to buy food.
They must buy it from the ruler.

But they do not know this ruler is
really Joseph. That is his secret.

Then Joseph tells his brothers his secret. Do you think they are happy?

Hebrew Slaves

Work, work, work! That's all the poor slaves did.

The king was mean to these slaves.
He made them work. But he did
not pay them.

But the slaves had something
wonderful! God gave them many
beautiful children.

The bad king did not like that.
So he planned to hurt these
beautiful children.

Baby Moses

Shhhh. Baby Moses is sleeping.
His mother hid him here.
Please don't wake him.

Some bad men want to hurt him.
If he cries, they may find him.

Look! A princess has found Baby Moses. She will take care of him.

Thank You, God.

A Bush Keeps Burning

"Help my people," Moses prayed.
Moses' people were slaves.

Then Moses saw a bush. It was burning. But it did not stop burning.

85

God talked to Moses. His voice
came from that burning bush.

"Lead your people from Egypt,"
God said. "I will help you."

Ten Bad Things

"Let my people go! Stop making them your slaves," Moses said. "No!" said the king.

Then bad things began to happen
to the king. God made these
things happen.

The king kept on saying NO!
God kept sending bad things to
hurt the king.

At last the king said YES. At last
he knew that God was greater
than his gods.

Moses Leads His People

The king wanted to keep Moses'
people. He wanted them to work
for him. These people were slaves.

Now Moses' people are going far
away. Moses will lead them and
God will lead Moses.

The people are not slaves now.
How happy they are.

"Thank You, God," said Moses.
"Thank You, God," said the people.

Cloud and Fire

Moses is leading his people.
He is leading them to a new
home far away.

But Moses has never been there.
How will he know where to go?

Look! Do you see what Moses sees?
There is a tall cloud. God leads
Moses with this cloud each day.

Now it is night. God leads Moses with fire like a cloud. Thank You, God.

99

Walking through a Sea

"We need to go over there," the
people said. But a sea was
between here and there.

"How will we get across?" the people asked. "God will help us," said Moses.

101

God sent a wind. It blew on the sea.
The wind blew the water apart.

God made a dry path through the
sea. Now the people can walk to
the other side.

103

God Gives Good Food

"We're hungry," the people said. No one had food. What would they eat?

"God will send food for you to eat,"
Moses told the people.

God sent special bread called
manna. The people were glad
for the manna.

Now the people had food to eat.
God gave them all they needed.

God Gives Good Rules

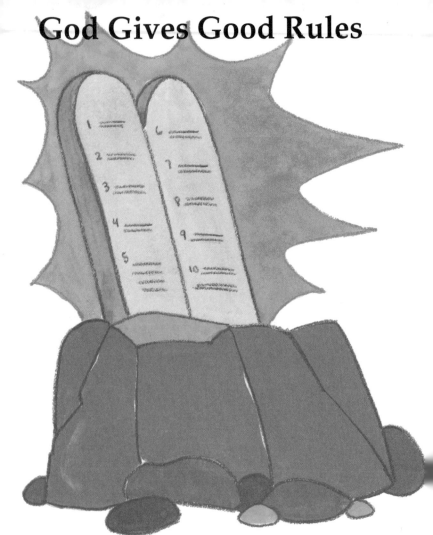

One day Moses went up into a mountain. God talked with him there.

"Here are some good rules,"
God said. "I want the people to
obey them."

Moses listened to God. Then he told the people what God said.

Some people obeyed God's rules.
That made them very happy.

The Golden Calf

One day Moses went away.
He wanted to talk with God.

Then some people made a golden
statue. "We will follow the statue,
not God," they said.

Moses was angry at these people.
"Follow God, not this statue,"
he said.

Some people listened to Moses.
They followed God. That made
them happy.

Giving to God

"God wants us to make a beautiful tent house for Him," Moses said.

The people gave many good gifts
to build God's tent house.

The people were happy to give
to God. They gave more than
Moses needed.

"Stop giving!" said Moses.
"We have enough to make God's
beautiful house."

119

God's Tent House

Look! Do you see that beautiful tent house? It was God's house. It was called a tabernacle.

Moses and his people made it.
They used the gifts the people
brought.

121

The beautiful tent had gold
furniture inside.

God talked with Moses in the
tabernacle. He told Moses how
to please Him.

123

God Gives Meat to Eat

"We're hungry," the people said.
"We want meat to eat."

There were no stores in the desert.
There was no place to get meat.

One day God sent quail. They flew down so the people could catch them.

Now the people had meat to eat.
God gave it to them.

God Promises a New Home

"Go into that land," God said.
"I will give it to you."

"We can't," said some men.
"The people are too big."

"We can," said other men. "God
will help us. He promised!"

But the people would not go in.
So they lived in the desert for a
long time. They were very sad.

The Walls of Jericho

Look at Jericho's walls! They are
so tall. How can Joshua capture
that city?

God told him how. "March around
the city," God said. "Obey Me."

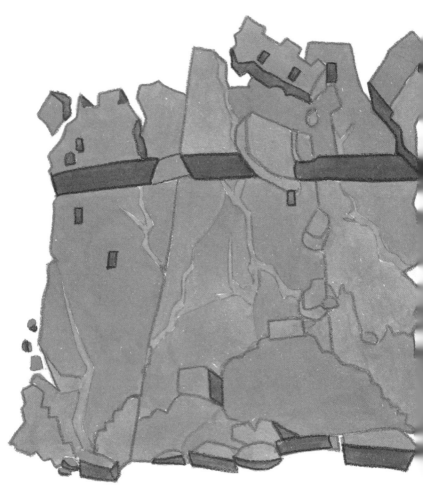

Joshua and his soldiers obeyed.
They marched around the city the
way God said.

At last the walls of Jericho fell
down. Joshua and his soldiers
went into the city.

Gideon's Little Army

Gideon had a little army.
The Midianites had a big army.
But God was helping Gideon.

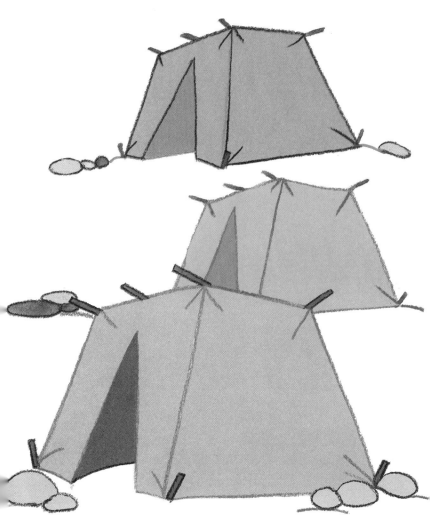

One night God said, "Light torches
and cover them with pitchers.
Go near the enemy camp."

Gideon and his little army obeyed.
"Break the pitchers," God said.
The torches shined in the darkness.

The Midianites saw the torches. They
heard Gideon's soldiers shouting. So
the big army was afraid and ran away.

Samson Fights a Lion

Samson was the strongest man in the world. God made him strong.

One day a lion jumped at Samson.
What would Samson do?

Then God helped Samson.
He gave Samson great strength.

Samson grabbed the lion's mouth.
He killed the lion with his hands.
God really did help him, didn't He?

A Wonderful Lady Named Ruth

Ruth and Naomi lived together.
One day Naomi decided to go
home to Israel.

"I will go with you," said Ruth.
"Stay here with your own people,"
said Naomi.

145

But Ruth loved Naomi. So she left her people. She went with Naomi.

Naomi was too old to work. So
Ruth worked in the grain fields to
take care of her.

God Talks to Samuel

Do you see that golden chest? It is in God's house, the tabernacle.

The boy Samuel lives in God's house. He sleeps near this golden chest.

149

One night God talked to Samuel.
Samuel loved God. So he listened.

God told Samuel something special.
It is good to listen to God, isn't it?

A New King

Israel did not have a king.
God told Samuel what to say.
Then Samuel told the people.

But the people wanted a king. They
wanted to be like other nations.

"A king will take money from you,"
said Samuel. "He will make you
work hard for him."

"We want a king," the people said.
God helped Samuel choose a king.
He was a tall man named Saul.

David Fights a Giant

Look at that giant! His name is
Goliath. He wants to fight David.

How can David win? He has only
a slingshot. Goliath has a big spear.

But David asked God to help him.
Goliath did not ask God to help.

That's why David won.

David's New Friend

Who is that young man with the bow and arrows? He is Prince Jonathan!

Jonathan likes David. He saw
David knock that giant down.
He knew God had helped David.

Prince Jonathan is giving David many wonderful gifts. He wants to be David's best friend.

David and Jonathan became best friends for a long, long time.

David Helps Mephibosheth

Do you see Mephibosheth?
He is the one with crutches.

He is the son of King David's best
friend, Jonathan. So David wants
to be kind to him.

David gives Mephibosheth many good gifts. David tells him to live in the palace with him.

Do you think Mephibosheth said
"thank you" to King David?

A Special Gift for King Solomon

One night King Solomon had a
dream. God talked to him in
this dream.

"I will give you anything," God
said. He could ask for money.
He could ask to be a hero.

"Help me be a wise king," said
Solomon. "Help me rule my
people well."

God was pleased. "I will make you
wise," God said. "I will also make
you rich and famous."

Solomon Builds God's House

"What are you doing?" a boy asked. "Building God's house," said a man.

King Solomon wanted a beautiful
house for God. So he had workers
put it together.

At last God's house was built.
"Come to God's house," said
the king.

People came from all over the land.
King Solomon prayed. The people
sang. Everyone liked God's house.

Ravens Feed Elijah

"There is no water," people said.
It had not rained for a long time.

Plants did not grow without rain.
So there was no food to eat.

Elijah needed food too. But God
took care of His helper Elijah.
Each day God sent ravens.

Each day the ravens brought food
to Elijah. "Thank You, God," Elijah
said. God was taking care of him.

God Sends Food Every Day

"Please make bread for me," said Elijah. "But I have only a little flour," said the poor woman.

"God will give you flour," said Elijah.
The woman believed him. She made
some bread for Elijah.

Most people had no food.
But this woman always had
flour to make bread.

Do you think she was thankful?
"God sent you to help us," she
said to Elijah.

Who Is Really God?

"Baal is God!" some men said. They were bad men. They did not believe in God. Baal was only a little statue.

Some people believed Baal was God. Some knew that God was God.

"Who really is God?" Elijah asked.
He was God's helper. "Let the true
God send fire from heaven."

Of course a little statue could not
do that. But God did! So the people
knew that God was truly God.

A Room for Elisha

"Eat with us when you come to town," a man and woman said to Elisha.

Elisha went there often to eat.
One day the man and woman
had a surprise.

"Look at the beautiful room we have made for you," said the woman.

"Thank you," said Elisha. "And thank you for being God's helper," said the woman.

A Big Chest in God's House

"Fix God's house!" King Joash said. You see why it needed to be fixed, don't you?

But the priests needed money to
fix God's house. They needed to
pay workers to do it.

So the priests put a big chest in God's house. They made a hole in the lid of the chest.

People brought money. The priests put it into the chest. Soon they could fix God's house.

Nehemiah Builds Some Walls

Look at those piles of stones.
Long ago they were beautiful walls.

Nehemiah wanted to build those walls again. He asked some men to help him.

197

Other men did not want that.
They tried to stop Nehemiah.
But Nehemiah kept on building.

Soon the walls were built.
"Thank You, God," said Nehemiah.

Queen Esther

"She's beautiful!" people whispered. Queen Esther was the most beautiful lady in the land.

A bad man named Haman wanted
to kill the Jewish people. He did not
know that Esther was Jewish.

One day Esther told the king what
Haman wanted to do. The king was
angry. He punished that bad man.

Queen Esther was happy. She had
saved her people. Do you think she
thanked God for helping her?

The Story of Job

One day a man ran to Job. "Your children and animals have died," he said.

Then Job got sores all over him.
What would you do now?

Did Job get angry at God? No.
"God gave me all I had," said Job.
"I will still love Him."

God was pleased that Job still loved
Him. So He gave Job much more
than he had before.

The King's Food

Some soldiers captured Daniel and his friends. They are in a new land. They must help the new king.

"We will teach you," said the king's helper. "But you must eat what the king eats."

This food had been offered to the king's gods. Daniel should not eat that!

"Please let us have some other
food," said Daniel and his friends.
Do you think that pleased God?

Daniel and the Lions

Daniel loved God. He prayed to
God each day. God loved Daniel too.

Some bad men did not like Daniel.
They tricked the king. He said no
one could pray to God.

But Daniel would not stop
praying. So the king put Daniel
into a lions' den.

God shut the lions' mouths. He would not let them hurt Daniel. You're glad, aren't you?

215

Jonah and a Big Fish

"Go to Nineveh," God told Jonah.
But Jonah ran away. He went far
away on a ship.

God knew that Jonah was on the ship. So He sent a big storm.

The sailors were afraid. They
threw Jonah into the sea. Then
a big fish swallowed him.

God told the fish what to do.
The fish took Jonah back to land.
NOW Jonah went where God said!

Angel Brings
od News

Have you ever seen an angel?
Mary did. The angel talked to her.
He told her some good news.

"You will have a baby," the angel
said. "He will be God's Son.
You will call Him Jesus."

"I will do what God wants me to do," said Mary.

Then the angel was gone. Do you think Mary thanked God for His good news?

Baby Jesus

Shhh. Do you see the baby?
This is Baby Jesus.

Shhh. Do you see the animals?
Baby Jesus is sleeping in a manger.

Shhh. The people of Bethlehem
are asleep now. They do not
know that this is God's Son.

Shhh. Whisper a prayer to God now.
"Thank You, God, for sending Baby
Jesus."

Shepherds Visit Jesus

"Look! Is that an angel?" a shepherd asked. There WAS an angel in the sky.

The angel talked to the shepherd
and his friends. "Good news! God's
Son has been born in Bethlehem!"

The sky was filled with angels.
They sang and praised God.
Then they were gone.

The shepherds hurried to Bethlehem to see Baby Jesus. Would you like to have been there too?

Wise Men Visit Jesus

"We must follow the star," a Wise Man said. "Now," said the others.

The Wise Men rode camels far
from home. They went all the
way to Bethlehem.

"This is the place," they said.
"The new King is here!"

The Wise Men gave wonderful gifts
to little Jesus. That made them very
happy.

Going to Egypt

Could anyone not like little Jesus?
Yes. A bad king did not like Him.
He wanted to kill Jesus.

This bad king had soldiers.
"Kill Him!" the king said. So the
soldiers looked for little Jesus.

237

But an angel talked to Joseph. "Take
little Jesus to Egypt," the angel said.

So little Jesus lived in Egypt for a while. God took care of Him there.

The Boy Jesus

Who is that boy? He is making
something with wood.

Now you know! That boy is Jesus. He is helping Joseph. Joseph is a carpenter.

The Boy Jesus grew up in a little town called Nazareth. Mary and Joseph took care of Him there.

God took care of the Boy Jesus too.
Thank You, God.

Jesus Teaches Some Teachers

Do you see all those men? They are teachers in God's house, the temple.

But look! What is that boy doing?
Jesus is talking with these teachers.

"How does this boy know so
much about God?" the teachers
wondered. You know, don't you?

Mary and Joseph know too. Jesus is
God's Son. But now it is time for
Him to go home to Nazareth.

A Preacher Named John

That man doesn't look like a preacher.
But he is! His name is John.

John doesn't preach in a church.
He preaches out in a lonely desert.

But many people come to hear
him. They listen carefully. John
tells them about God.

Some want to follow God. They want to do what He wants. Now John is glad he preached to them.

John Baptizes Jesus

"I want to please God," some people said. John baptized them in the Jordan River.

Others watched John baptize them.
They knew now that these people
wanted to please God.

"Baptize Me," Jesus said to John one day. "I will please God too."

When John did that, God spoke.
"This is My Son!" God said.
"He really does please Me."

Jesus Is Tempted

Do you see Jesus? He is alone.
He has been in this lonely place
for 40 days.

But Jesus has not eaten all this time.
He is very hungry.

Look! There is Satan! He has come to tempt Jesus. He wants Jesus to obey him instead of God.

But Jesus will not obey Satan. "I must always obey God!" He said. Do you want to obey God too?

Nicodemus Visits Jesus

Do you see that man with Jesus?
That's Nicodemus. He is an
important teacher.

Nicodemus knew many things about God. But he knew that Jesus knew more than he did.

"Let God give you a new life!"
Jesus said. "It's like being born a
second time."

Nicodemus listened carefully.
Do you think he learned something
important that night?

263

A Woman at a Well

"Please give Me a drink," Jesus said to the woman. The woman stood by a well. She had some water.

Now you see the woman asking
Jesus many questions. She knows
He is someone very special.

"God's Son will come some day,"
the woman said. "He already has,"
said Jesus. "I am God's Son."

The woman ran back to her village.
"Come and see a special man I met,"
she said. "He must be God's Son!"

Jesus Goes Fishing

"Let's go fishing," Jesus said.
Simon Peter caught fish for a living.

"We fished all last night," Simon Peter answered. "But we didn't catch one fish."

Jesus smiled. "You will today!"
He said. "Put your nets over there!"

Now look at all those fish. Jesus made that happen. Only God's Son could do that.

Come with Me

Jesus was doing wonderful things.
But He wanted some helpers.

One day Jesus saw Simon Peter and his brother Andrew fishing. "Come with Me!" said Jesus.

The two men stopped fishing.
They went with Jesus. So did
their partners, James and John.

Now Jesus had four good helpers.
He would teach them many things.
And they would help do His work.

Down through the Roof

"Let us in!" four men shouted.
"We want Jesus to heal our friend."
But they could not get in.

You see the big crowd, don't you?
That's why the men can't get into
the house.

So the men climbed onto the roof.
They made a big hole. They let
their friend down to Jesus.

"I will heal your friend," Jesus said.
And He did! "Thank You, thank
You," said the four friends.

Jesus Calls Matthew

People didn't like Matthew. He
made them pay taxes to the Romans.

The Romans had captured this
land. So the people there hated
them.

But Jesus wanted Matthew to be
His helper. "Follow Me!" He said.

Matthew left his good job. He would be very happy doing Jesus' work.

Jesus Chooses Twelve Helpers

"I want twelve of you to do special work for Me," said Jesus.

There were many helpers with Jesus
that day. But Jesus chose twelve to
do special work.

These twelve would be called The
Twelve Disciples. They would help
Jesus in special ways.

"Thank You, Jesus," the twelve men must have said. "Thank You for letting us be Your special helpers."

Jesus Preaches a Sermon

Look at all those people! They have come to hear Jesus preach.

Look at that tall hill! That's where
Jesus will preach to the people.
We should listen too.

Listen! Do you hear what Jesus is saying? He is telling us how to follow Him. Listen to Him.

Jesus says we must be like Him.
We must do what He would do.
We must do what He says. Will you?

A Widow's Boy

Why is that poor woman crying?
Oh! Now you can see! Her boy has
died. Those people will bury him.

But look! Here comes Jesus.
What do you think He will do?

"Please don't cry," said Jesus. Then He touched the boy's coffin. "Get up!" Jesus said to the boy.

The boy got up. He is not dead
now! Jesus brought him back to life.
That's why the woman is so happy.

295

Jesus' Wonderful Stories

Everyone wants to hear Jesus.
He has wonderful stories to tell.

Be careful, people! You don't want to push Jesus into the lake, do you?

That's better. Jesus knew what to do.
He can preach from that boat now.

Now Jesus will tell wonderful stories. The stories will tell us how to live for God.

Jesus Stops a Storm

Look at those big waves. Do you
see the boat bobbing on the big
waves?

Now you see who is in the boat. It's Jesus' friends. But where is Jesus?

"Wake up, Jesus!" His friends shout. Jesus was asleep in the boat. "Help us," they cry.

"Stop storm," Jesus said. The storm stopped. Even a storm obeys God's Son. Do you?

Jairus' Daughter

"Help me!" Jairus said. "My daughter is sick." Jesus went with Jairus.

But look at all those people crying.
Jairus' daughter has already died.

"Get up, little girl," Jesus said.
What do you think will happen
now?

Look! She's up! Jairus' daughter is
alive again. Only Jesus could do that.

Lunch for 5,000

Do you see all those people?
There are 5,000 fathers and
mothers and children.

Those people are hungry.
They have been here for a long
time, listening to Jesus.

309

But no one brought lunch except
one little boy. "May I have your
lunch?" Jesus asked.

Do you know what Jesus did with the boy's lunch? He fed all those people. Only Jesus could do that.

Jesus Walks on Water

Do you see the men in that little boat? They are in trouble. They are afraid their boat will sink.

"Help!" the men shout. But who can help them?

The men see someone walking on
the water. It is Jesus! He is coming
toward them.

314

Jesus gets into the boat. Shhh, wind.
Shhh, waves. This is God's Son.
Look how quiet they become.

315

Jesus Is Our Good Shepherd

Do you see that shepherd with his sheep? He loves his sheep. He takes good care of them.

"I am your Good Shepherd," Jesus told His friends. He is our Good Shepherd too.

Jesus loves us like the shepherd
loves his sheep. He takes care of
us like a good shepherd should.

318

Thank You, Jesus, for loving me.
Thank You, Jesus, for taking good
care of me.

319

Mary and Martha

Mary and Martha are Jesus' friends.
They are glad that He has come to
see them today.

Mary has so many things to ask Jesus. It is wonderful to hear Him talk about God and His home.

Martha doesn't have time to talk.
She is too busy getting dinner.
"Make Mary help me," Martha say

Jesus smiled. "It's more important
to talk about God than to eat
dinner," He said. Do you think so?

The Lost Sheep

This shepherd has 100 sheep. But he loves each one of them. He feeds them. He takes care of them.

One day the shepherd has only 99
sheep. One of them is lost. What
will this shepherd do?

The shepherd loves that little lost
lamb. So he looks for it until he
finds it. He is so happy!

"I love you like a little lost lamb,"
Jesus said. "I am so happy
when I can help you find God."

A Boy Who Ran Away

"Give me some money," a boy told his father. "I want to leave home. I want to do things my way now."

The father was sad. But he gave the boy some money. Then the boy went far away. He spent all the money.

Now the boy is alone and hungry.
He wants to go home. Will his
father let him do that?

Yes, you can see that he does. He forgives his boy. God forgives us too when we ask Him. Will you?

Lazarus Is Alive!

Do you see Mary and Martha crying? Their brother Lazarus has died. They are so sad.

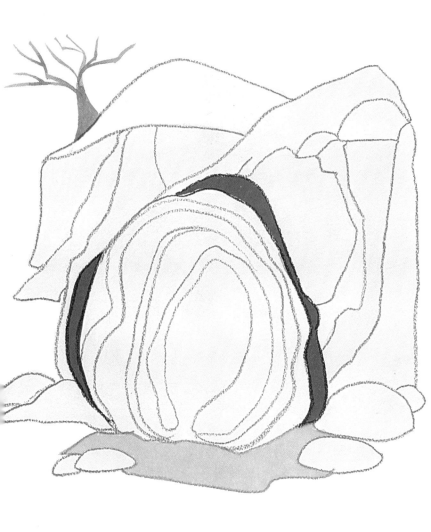

But look. Here comes Jesus. He has
come to the place where Lazarus is
buried. What will He say now?

"Lazarus! Come out of there!" Jesus shouts. That's Lazarus coming out of the tomb. He's alive again!

Only God's Son could make a dead person live again. Aren't you glad Jesus is your friend?

Ten Men with Terrible Trouble

Ten men had terrible trouble.
They were very sick. They had
leprosy. They had terrible sores.

These men could not live with other
people. They had to go far away.
They could not touch anyone else.

"Help us, Jesus!" these men begged.
Then Jesus healed them. "Thank
You, Jesus," said one man.

But the others forgot to say "thank You." Have you said "thank You" to Jesus today? Would you like to now?

Jesus Loves Children

Shhh. Do you hear what Jesus is saying?

"Let the children come to Me,"
Jesus says.

The children are coming to Jesus.
Do you see them? They want to
be with Jesus.

Do you like to talk with Jesus? He wants you to. Remember to do that today. He loves you.

Blind Bartimaeus

"Please help me," Bartimaeus shouted. In Jesus' time, blind people had to beg for money.

Kind people gave Bartimaeus
money. "Thank you, thank you,"
he said.

One day Jesus came along the road
"Please help me," Bartimaeus
shouted. "I will!" said Jesus.

Now Bartimaeus is not blind. He sees Jesus smiling at him. "Thank You, thank You!" he whispers.

Zacchaeus

Once there was a short little man named Zacchaeus. He wanted to see Jesus when He came to town.

There was a big crowd around
Jesus. All those people were too tall.
Zacchaeus could not see over them.

Look where Zacchaeus went.
He's up in the tree. Jesus sees him.

"Come down," said Jesus. "I want
to talk with you." Zacchaeus was so
happy to talk with Jesus. Are you?

Jesus Rides into Jerusalem

Who is riding on that donkey?
It's Jesus! He will ride into the
big city named Jerusalem.

"Praise God," people shout. They throw palm branches and cloaks on the path where Jesus will ride.

Look at that crowd. They are shouting. They are singing. The people want Jesus to be their king.

But Jesus is more important than any king. He rules over all the world. Jesus is God's Son.

A Woman's Big-Little Gift

"Look," Jesus said. His friends saw a poor woman. She was giving two little coins at God's house.

Jesus' friends also saw some rich men. They gave lots of money.

"That woman gave more than
those rich men," said Jesus.
"She gave all that she had."

Jesus wants us to give our best to Him. You will, won't you?

The Last Supper

What is Jesus doing? He's breaking that piece of bread. He will give it to His friends.

This is a special supper. It is the last supper Jesus will have with His friends.

"Remember Me," He said.
"Remember how I will die for you."

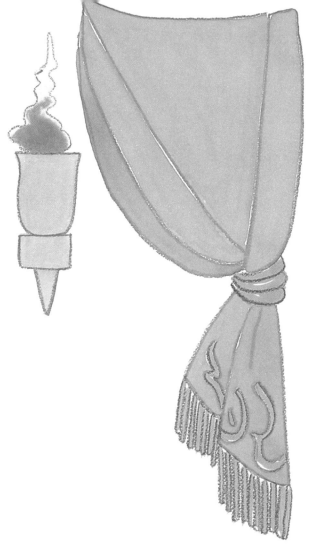

Do you have communion in your church? People remember Jesus when they eat and drink at that time.

Jesus Prays in a Garden

"Wait here," Jesus said to three friends.
"I must go over there and pray."

Jesus' friends watched. He went to
a big rock. He bowed His head.
Then He began to pray.

"Father, help Me do what You want," Jesus prayed.

That's a good prayer for us to pray too, isn't it?

Jesus Dies on the Cross

Some men are nailing Jesus to a big wooden cross. He has not hurt them. But look what they are doing.

Jesus died that day on the cross. He
came to earth to do this. That's
because He loves us so much.

Jesus wants to help us live with God in heaven. When we sin, we can't go there.

But Jesus died to take away our sin.
He wants to be our Saviour. He will
if we ask. Will you ask Him?

Some Women Visit Jesus' Tomb

There is an angel! Do you see it?
The angel is talking to Jesus' friends.

"He has risen!" the angel says.
"Jesus is alive again! Come and see
where His body was lying."

The women go into the tomb.
The angel is right. Jesus is not there
He has risen from the dead.

Now there is another angel! "Go and
tell the Good News," the angel says.
That's what the women will do.

Jesus Goes Back to Heaven

Jesus and His friends are walking to the top of a mountain. It is called the Mount of Olives.

"The Holy Spirit will soon come,"
Jesus tells them. "Then you will tell
people everywhere about Me."

Then something exciting happens.
Jesus is rising up into the sky. He
goes all the way back to heaven.

Two angels speak. "Jesus has gone
back to heaven," they say. "Some
day He will come back."

The Holy Spirit Comes

Shhh. Jesus' friends are praying.
They are together in a room upstairs
But look!

There is a little fire on each person's
head. But the fire doesn't hurt.
What is happening?

These friends know. Jesus told
them. The Holy Spirit has come.
He will help them do great things.

Now they will tell people
everywhere about Jesus. The Holy
Spirit will help us do that too.

An Ethiopian Hears about Jesus

Here comes a chariot. Do you see
the man in it? He is a very
important man from Ethiopia.

This man is reading God's Word.
Philip will help him know God's
Word better.

Philip tells the man what God's
Word says about Jesus. Now the
man wants to become Jesus' friend

This man accepted Jesus. He became Jesus' friend. Now he will tell many in Ethiopia about Jesus.

387

Saul Becomes Jesus' Friend

That man Saul is a mean man. He hates Jesus' friends. He is going to another city to hurt them.

Suddenly a bright light shines. It is
coming from heaven. Someone in
heaven talks to Saul.

"I am Jesus!" the voice says. "You are hurting Me. Stop it! I want you to be My helper."

Saul knows now that Jesus is God's Son. He will stop hurting Jesus. He will help Jesus do His work.

391

Barnabas Is a Good Friend

Saul needs a friend. His old friends hate him. Saul follows Jesus now. His old friends do not like that.

But Jesus' followers are still afraid
of Saul. He hurt many of them
before he accepted Jesus.

"I will be your friend." Barnabas told Saul.

Now Barnabas' friends are Saul's friends too. They will help Saul tell many others about Jesus.

Dorcas Is Alive Again

Dorcas was a special lady. She was always helping someone. She cooked. She sewed. She did many things.

396

Everyone loved Dorcas. But one day Dorcas died. Her friends were so sad.

"Find Peter!" her friends said. "He will help us." So someone found Peter. He came to Dorcas' house.

"Get up, Dorcas," Peter said. Then
Dorcas was alive again. How happy
all her friends were!

Singing in Jail

Do you remember Saul?
People call him Paul now.
He and Silas are in jail.

Some bad men put them there.
But Paul and Silas are singing.
They sing about Jesus, even in jail.

Suddenly God shakes the jail.
The doors fly open. Paul and Silas
can run away. But they don't.

The man in charge knows they could
have run away. But they didn't.
Now he wants to follow Jesus too.

Telling a King about Jesus

Do you see that king and his sister? People were afraid of a king. He might not like what they said.

A king could hurt them or kill
them. Will Paul tell the king about
Jesus? Will he be afraid?

405

"I wish you would become a
Christian," Paul told the king.
"I wish you would accept Jesus."

Paul told everyone about Jesus.
He wanted everyone he met to
accept Jesus. Do you?

Shipwreck!

This ship is in trouble. The people
on the ship are in trouble too.
Do you see the stormy sea?

The ship is taking Paul far away.
A king will decide if Paul should
be killed.

Oh, no! The ship has crashed on some rocks. What will happen to Paul and the other men?

God takes care of Paul and the others. No one is hurt. God has special things for Paul to do.

411

A Boy Named Timothy

Timothy's mother helped him love
God's word.

So did his grandmother.

Does someone help you love God's word? You're happy when they do.

Jesus is happy too!